MOTOC S

STAFFORDSHIRE LIBRARY AND INFORMATION SERVICES
Please return or renew by the last date shown

PERT

PERTON

If not required by other readers, this item may may be renewed
in person, by post or telephone, online or by email.
To renew, either the book or ticket are required

24 HOUR RENEWAL LINE 0845 33 00 740

CLASH

STAFFORDSHIRE LIBRARIES

3 8014 09165 6519

Copyright © ticktock Entertainment Ltd 2008

First published in Great Britain in 2008 by ticktock Media Ltd,
The Old Sawmill, 103 Goods Station Road, Tunbridge Wells, Kent, TN1 2DP

ticktock project editor: Ruth Owen
ticktock project designer: Sara Greasley
ticktock picture researcher: Lizzie Knowles

With thanks to series editors Honor Head and Jean Coppendale

Thank you to Lorraine Petersen and the members of nasen

ISBN 978 1 84696 708 5 pbk

Printed in China
9 8 7 6 5 4 3 2

A CIP catalogue record for this book is available from the British Library.
No part of this publication may be reproduced, copied, stored in a retrieval system or transmitted in any form or
by any means electronic, mechanical, photocopying, recording or otherwise without prior written permission of
the copyright owner.

Picture credits (t=top; b=bottom; c=centre; l=left; r=right):
Steve Bardens/ actionplus: 4-5, 21b. Shelly Castellano/ Icon SMI/ Corbis: 26-27. DPPI/ Actionplus: 29. Imagebroker/
Alamy: 25t. Ben Johnson: 10-11. Martin Meissner/ AP/ PA Photos: 12-13. Aris Messinis/ AFP/ Getty Images: 24-25. Phil
Rees/ Rex Features: 23. Sherman/ Getty Images: 7. Shutterstock: OFC, 1, 2, 8, 14, 15, 16, 17, 18-19, 19t, 20, 21t, 28, 31.

Every effort has been made to trace copyright holders, and we apologise in advance for any omissions. We would be pleased to
insert the appropriate acknowledgments in any subsequent edition of this publication.

CONTENTS

WARNING!

The moves and stunts featured in this book have been performed by experienced, highly-trained motocross riders. Under no circumstances try them yourself. **You have been warned!**

Neither the publisher nor the author shall be liable for any bodily harm or damage to property whatsoever that may be caused or sustained as a result of conducting any of the activities featured in this book.

THE START

Motocross is one of the most exciting sports in the world.

Up to 40 riders on special motorbikes race against each other.

They race on dirt tracks in open country. A motocross track is about 1,500 to 2,000 metres long.

The tracks include huge hills and drops. There are fast, bumpy straights and tight corners.

There are big jumps.

This is motocross!

FLASHBACK

The first motocross races took place in the 1940s.

Special bikes were built for motocross from old road motorbikes.

The first motocross tracks didn't have many jumps because the bikes were heavy and not very strong. Also, the bikes had very poor acceleration. But on a straight, the bikes could go at about 130 km/h.

Tracks were built to be as fast as possible. They had lots of straights and fast corners.

The first motocross bikes were made entirely of metal. Sometimes they weighed 200 kilograms!

Modern motocross bikes weigh about 100 kilograms.

MIGHTY MACHINES

Over the years, motocross bikes have developed more powerful engines.

They have tougher suspension and are much lighter. Modern bikes are made from lightweight aluminium and tough plastic.

This means the tracks can be rougher! They have more jumps and bigger jumps.

Modern tracks test the riders to the limit.

In the 1980s and 1990s, motocross became more and more popular. Today, thousands of people all over the world watch and take part in motocross races.

THE BIKE

Motocross bikes are very different from normal motorbikes. The engines are built for power and speed.

The 2008 Yamaha YZ250F is one of the best and most powerful motocross bikes.

It has six gears.

It has 33 centimetres of suspension at the front and back. This soaks up the impact of the big jumps and rough bumps on the track.

Slim bodywork

Chunky tread

Lightweight frame

Powerful engine

Tough suspension

Tyres with a chunky tread help
the bike to grip the loose dirt.

IT'S TOUGH!

Motocross is one of the toughest sports in the world. Riders must train hard.

Riders must be very fit and strong to compete.

Sometimes bad crashes happen!

SAFETY GEAR

Riders wear lots of special gear and clothing when they race.

A helmet protects the head in a crash. It stops dirt and rocks hitting the face. Goggles protect the eyes.

Helmet

Goggles

Armour is worn under or over a rider's jersey. It protects their chest and back from flying dirt and crashes.

Riders wear special race jerseys, gloves and jeans. They are made of tough material. It is very light. It lets the rider move easily and not become too hot.

Knee braces protect their knees in a fall.

Riders wear leather boots with hard plastic protectors. The boots keep their feet and legs safe from damage in falls, and from other riders!

THE RACE

Racers live for the time they line up for the start of a race.

The starter holds up a 30-second board. There are **30 seconds** to go before the race starts.

The starter holds up another board. There are **5 seconds** to go. The riders get their bikes in gear.

OTOCROSS TRACK IN THE WORL

RIA · SEVLIEVO

Then they are off!

The racers charge into the first turn together.
The bikes must pull through the deep dirt. This is
the most exciting and dangerous part of the race.

SPEED AND SKILL

The early stages of a race are frantic. Riders fight over top positions.

The bikes power up fast to push over the jumps.

Only the most skilful riders are able to attack the track and different jumps at full speed.

They quickly find their way to the front.

THE FINISH

The race lasts for 30 minutes. The track gets very rough at the end of the race.

The riders start to feel physically tired and mentally tired.

Riders who have trained hard and are fitter, pass tired rivals. They can keep up their speed and overtake.

For some riders tiredness means they come off their bikes and crash into the mud.

What does it take to win?

Focus
Energy
Strength
Talent
Skill

and maybe some
Good luck!

SUPERCROSS

Supercross is a more spectacular form of motocross racing.

It takes place on specially built tracks, inside big stadiums.

Supercross is all about huge jumps and tight turns. These make the races more exciting and scary, and wow the huge crowds.

The races are short and action-packed. Racers have to ride very hard to overtake and get a good finish. Big crashes sometimes happen.

The tracks are smaller than normal motocross tracks.

Stadium

Track

Racers

23

JUMPS

Supercross jumps need perfect timing.

The jumps give riders lots of chances to overtake. As they fly over the jumps, riders try to take a better route than their rivals and overtake them.

Long sections of jumps are called rhythm sections. The closely spaced bumps are known as whoops.

This is a big triple jump.
Triple jumps throw riders high into the air side-by-side.

Rhythm section

Whoops

FREESTYLE

Freestyle is the most extreme type of motocross. It's also the most dangerous.

Riders do not race in freestyle. Instead they perform giant leaps and amazing tricks on their bikes.

Take-off ramp

They do these giant leaps on specially built
ramps, or off huge natural jumps and hills.

TRICKS

Good freestyle riders often do more than one trick as they fly through the air.

Here a freestyle rider performs two tricks at once. This move is called a **Seat Grab Hart Attack.**

A **Seat Grab** is when a rider grabs hold of the bike's saddle.

A **Hart Attack** is when a rider throws his or her legs into the air above their head. This trick was invented by rider Carey Hart.

A rider gets upside down as he performs
the **Backflip**. This is one of the hardest
and most dangerous freestyle tricks of all.
Only the best riders can tackle this move.

Motocross really is incredible!

NEED TO KNOW WORDS

acceleration The rate at which a bike increases its speed.

drop A steep slope from the top of a hill. Drops make the track more challenging.

gears Mechanical parts of the bike. They help it to accelerate. They also produce more power when powering up for jumps.

rhythm sections Long sections of jumps with different size spaces in between.

straight The fastest section of a motocross track. Straights are not long, but they are difficult to ride. This is because the ground is rough so the riders must hang on tight.

suspension The suspension is one of the most important parts of a motocross bike. It acts like a cushion so the riders don't feel all the bumps of the track. It also helps the tyres grip the track.

tread The surface of a tyre. The tread on motocross tyres has thick rubber blocks. They dig into the dirt to push the bike forwards and stop the wheels spinning.

triple jump When riders jump a huge distance in the air over a jump that features three dirt ramps in a row. The best riders jump all three ramps in one go.

whoops A section of track that features a long series of big man-made bumps. The riders attack them at speed so they can skim across the top of the bumps.

BE A RACER

- Getting started in motocross is easier than you think. Each week, boys and girls line up together all over the world to ride and compete in races. Riders can take part in races from as young as 4 years old!

- The Auto-Cycle Union (ACU) has a list of companies that will teach you to ride motocross. See their website – *http://www.acu.org.uk*

MOTOCROSS ONLINE

Websites

http://www.motocrossmx1.com

http://www.mxgb.co.uk

http://www.womensmotocrossassociation.com

http://www.acu.org.uk

INDEX